Play Lists

Mo

ISBN: 978-1-913642-51-8

Book designed by Aaron Kent

Edited by Aaron Kent

Broken Sleep Books (2021), Talgarreg, Wales

Contents

Play Lists

Jessica Mookherjee

"With Myself, Always Myself, Never Forgetting"

– Tracey Emin

Talking

Your mind flows over each neuron and bursts
into a star flower as I watch, all lost for words,
talk unprepared, thick and after hours
you ask me who I am—I wish you were less

familiar, your question helps me lose feral notes
of what comes next; words that stick,
that glow with what comes from being sea sick,
changes in one drift of instant. I wish

I'd not had that last drink, where the wine glass
grows bright, I say oh no oh no it's out of my hands
spilt over sawdust of a south London pub floor
and my dress. We talk and talk about Lacan.

Hero Worship

Achilles picked me up from school in his red sports car.
My spring term, buds out, shirt buttons
undone, skirt hitched up. *Get in* he said, sounding American,
I swooned as the girls turned. He looked through our smiles,
and told me in a whisper that I looked like Lydia Lunch.

I walked down hallways looking for him, wrote his name
on my pencil case, swore blind, made excuses, like some poor fool,
spent my days cutting him out of magazines. He was drunk
with Pat in the dark dive bars near the station, where I found him.
He told me in a whisper I was wasting my time.

So I got all love bitten on a sugar-coated neck as he sent
me love songs on the internet, hired a man to write my name
in the sky with a plane, *take me back*. I smiled
as he bled from his heals, showed things to Pat no girl
can reveal. It was spring and my step had a mean, mean streak.

The girls, creamed up with strawberry lip-gloss, crossed their legs
in bobby-socks, watched me out of the sides of their eyes.
Achilles picked me up on his motor bike, outside the school gates, down
narrow lanes, on lines of speed and acid tabs. It was April,
he told me I was a cruel, cruel girl to tease him like that.

Stalker

I didn't want you to hold my hand or even like me. But you were
funny, I liked your gang and the way you used to walk me home
from school, though the way you followed me about the corridors
unnerved me, I didn't know why. You were everywhere I looked. I
admitted that you made me laugh. You cried tears and said
you liked the things I did; said everything I did delighted you. I
didn't want to be seen with you but your face was sensational, you
got me listening to those bold bad drums and boot stomping songs
and taught me about riffs and how they could put heart break and
dirt into a song and then spoiled everything by holding my hand.
You stood up and kissed me in front of everyone. I almost died
when you declared undying love and when they expected us to get
married. My mother stopped me seeing you and I was relieved. You
waited for me outside my house, everyday, telling me this would
lead to better things, there would be a world where it wouldn't
matter that my parents were from Bangladesh and yours from
Wolverhampton. I said you were catchy but not a catch, and mostly
ignored you, wished you wouldn't turn up every Christmas. Though
in secret sometimes I wondered how you were getting on – someone
told me years later you'd become a skinhead and a hooligan, and
into English Rose but I didn't really believe it. You were the first to
love me. Years later when I saw a picture of you I was shocked, you
were certainly not as good looking as I remember.

Hell for Leather

Too much air in your lungs, too much orange food colouring and sugar,
we spent money on all the multi-coloured sherbet in the village shops,
tongues twisted and purple green – we yelled all the way home.

At first you tried your hand at being cool, I hung back, consumed
with a sugar-rush, fizzing to get closer to you. then you tried making fun
of me, and I frowned and laughed at the same time. You came too close

and pulled my hair. Spoiled everything, as you strutted Jagger-lipped,
vacant, and I followed you home. Here was leather belt, a sword hung
from your bedroom window, you said you were a Viking devil.

You started clapping and stomping at the same time as you waxed
lyrical until I got tired of waiting for you to let me speak. *Touch
this jacket on pain of death* you said and I placed its tasselled chords

in my grubby-sticky fingers and pulled. You were trapped for a second
as your voice broke from falsetto to growl. I said your sweat smelled.
You told me I wasn't in your band anymore because I was a girl.

Sidekick

We graduated from potato guns to plastic lugers, you were always the hero,
You can be the hero's girlfriend you said and gave me the rubbish gun. You said
you were Logan 5 and I had to be Jessica 6. We graduated to kissing
in playing fields. You took me by surprise that summer, we found punk records
we liked in HMV. *Why won't you let me kiss your lips?* You kept saying,
I didn't know the answer, the feel of you on my neck was enough. You
yelled into the sea, that summer, got your armour all wet. You climbed
out of the waves, dripping with salt water, I was on the rocks pretending
to smoke. You slipped in some sea weed
as I shot you with that cap-gun between the eyes. You said I was mental,
a freak wave of nature. I said you were a one hit wonder.

Long Walk Home

These are bleak times he wrapped a heavy coat around himself,
said there was a band playing in Gorseinon – did I want to come,
I had no way of getting there without some assistance and would it be safe?
There is nothing safe, there are nuclear missiles about to go off,
don't you know what capitalism is? Don't you know where Mordor is?
I told him I did know – and could I have a lift? He said he wanted to
put make up on and could I help. I was ruby lips and pixie boots.
He was cut off denim jacket and a face of silver and green.
Your mascara is running, I told him. He sighed, *It's meant to look*
like this, get in the car or we'll be late. I was sandwiched
inside a bohemian rhapsody of boys. These were indeed bleak times.

Rolling Thunder

We started off as a good team. You said I could be your manager,
you were a wizard on the keyboards. You had sights set on big things.
I kept thinking of tidal waves, you knew all about Leap Tides.
We sat arm in arm on the sea's edge where your tongue tasted of salt,
I've written a song, I might dedicate it to you. It's quite Elton John.
I wanted Rocket Man, a painted boy from outer space with your cheekbones
and pretty face. You made me a doll from grass on the sandbank, as I rolled
a joint. Your perfect impressions of the teachers, we didn't stop laughing.
Until I said I didn't like any of your band names. You said you
wouldn't kiss me again, my lips were covered in hot wax and tasted of
Malteasers. My spiky hair bothered you, too pretentious, my shoes too
sharp and my eyes moving sideways.
A man in a leather jacket and a quiff walked passed us and blew me a kiss.
I blushed as he winked and signalled to the swings with his head.
I guess that's why they call it the blues; you said as you walked away,
the song I've written for you, it's a bit like that. I was too stoned to stand.

Dry.

We practiced smoking together, I got a packet of black menthol More
and you stole twenty Camels because you thought Jack Kerouac
smoked them but I thought it was Marlboro.

This is the end, my beautiful friend you sang, dressed in black.
We sloped across the beach where wind blew sand into our lipstick
the smoke blinded us and it rained. *This is shit* – you spat.

I didn't say anything but wondered which bit was bad. *I want to take
you in these caves* – you were trying to be menacing, your sunglasses
were broke and your hair was distressed.

I told you I had bought a new LP by Tin Tin Duffy and you practical-
ly
choked, *that's shit pop music* you said. *I like pop music* I said.
At least you're over your stupid Prog Rock phase then – he flared his lips.

I looked into the waves trying not to cry and he appeared at my side,
kissed me on my lips so many times, *It's too cold here
shall we go inside?* We found a deserted beach hut where he poured

out two glasses of cheap white wine. *We can get pissed and dance
to the sound of the waves and me beating on the rocks with my sticks.*
I felt sick but couldn't show it.

Nevermore

He saw dark flagged ships in me, before anyone else,
Let me catch them for you and they can be our friends.
There were always boys like that, the ones who didn't
play football. Some hints of the devil in him too.
We didn't speak much. I had a raven on my shoulder,
he walked a wolf down the promenade and told
me about serial killers and Charles Manson.
Between us, we knew nothing about heroin
or alcoholics or amphetamines but he had a book
by William Boroughs called Junky, told me to read it.
I read twelve pages and abandoned it, he devoured.
I wasn't allowed to talk to him in school but could meet
up by the woods where he'd give me a tape of all the songs
I should listen to, ones that had the sound of machines,
static, feedback. I turned up with a copy of Melody Maker
and Smash Hits to discuss what they'd written about Lou Reed.
He turned up with half a bottle of Jim Beam, sat on a tree stump,
smoking and read out the lyrics to *Berlin* as if they were poems,
told me his mother had left and started to cry. I saw gunboats
harboured in his chest, I felt echoes of a man I hadn't met.
He asked me first, before anyone else, and the raven
whispered *Go home, this isn't your adventure yet.*

Crush

The sun and air were your best friends, you were cool
breezes at the back of the class with them,
they didn't get your jokes but I laughed. I was at the front
taking notes. Heartbeat like a sickening ship as you put
an arm round my neck at break and asked
why I hadn't been to school for weeks. The other boys
distracted looking down Lucy King's shirt, you kissed
my hand and asked if I was into the Smiths.
Those lunch breaks dancing in the playing fields
waving bits of grass, twigs and flowers, sprawled
with our over long jumpers as we laughed. *You're the only one
I know that think's they're funny, I mean who says
'heaven knows' anyway?* So we kept our shaded secrets
until I knew the weight of the summer crushed me.

Cracked Actors

That summer I became Puck, Miranda, Titania,
you turned Romeo, Hamlet and Antonio.
Let's run away you said. *Peter Pan the fuck
out of here.* You stole your dad's Vauxhall Cavalier,
I stole my dad's chequebook, and we drank as you drove
down the motorway. I was in love with Bowie and you
were amused and jealous as I sang along to Diamond Dogs,
Sweet Thing and Five Years. You said I was beautiful
so I shaved off my eyebrows and spiked up my hair
and cupid-blind, I knew you were desperate. I stood
on the hotel room's bed with fish nets, a fake fur jacket,
painted lips of dust-ruby to take you. In the mirror we melted
together. Show reel slow, *is it hunky dory*? I wanted to know.
The tape recorder we bought on the way played Lady
Stardust. We acted like movie stars. Nothing was safe.
You were slicked back, I waxed and waned, made up
from a strange thing of you. Someone clapped, did we
make it from the bones and blood of us? All smeared
like lipstick on the sheets as we fell to earth.
The theatre lights dimmed, and we drove slow paced,
I was a vixen when I was back at school. You, Oberon,
had a line or too to get through. I was playing
kitchen sinks and gin until you were out of my system.

Fashionable Victim

after David Sylvian

There was a girl covered in chalk,
would that ever cross your mind?
Who fell for the boy in the lipstick and skirt,
down by the sorry tide.

His bearded brother came to call,
would that ever cross your mind?
He beat down the door and walls of her hut,
down by the sorry tide.

Her face was all but rubbed away,
Would that ever cross your mind?
His driving hands came through her tracks
down by the sorry tide.

She pined for the beautiful boy.
Would that ever cross your mind?
While his brother bragged in the local pub
down by the sorry tide.

She waited with a sharpened blade,
would that ever cross your mind?
and ripped a dead child from his chest
down by the sorry tide.

She took to wearing mourning robes,
would that ever cross your mind?
While she spent her time in the record shops
down by the sorry tide,

the beautiful boy was swept away.
Would that ever cross your mind?
She danced in the club for his quiet life
down by the sorry tide.

Now the child hides inside her guts,
would that ever cross your mind?
The music's become her Geisha girl
down by the sorry tide.

The Airman

His shock of curls and lips of a girl
unfurled as he winked and asked me out

for a drive in his new car, from headland
to a heartland, a picnic of strawberries.

His airman leather jacket, aviator glasses
wore languid, we talked about Camus,

self harm and suicide. Learned the lyrics
by heart, before we saw The Bad Seeds play.

I wrote on silence, he sang to the sound
of the car. *Safe, keep me safe* I asked the sun.

There was no one to catch me as I fell outside
his Belsize Park bedsit one night.

I prayed to him because he looked like Apollo
and when he changed gear, turned Odin.

Ask me, ask me I asked the sky, to *move in
and be your wife, all those normal things.*

He had a shock when I showed him my insides
and what they did. We drank vodka and lime

to still the pain of looking at brilliant lights
and walked round Kensington Market

where I was bad and uncivilised, he was good,
we were played, there, where I turned Laurel Tree.

Gentleman Thief

You knocked on my door, kissed the back of my hand,
slid, cunning, through night blue lights and wet pavements.
Arrived in a top hat, gloves and ripped up shoes, a few ounces
for personal use, reciting poems and the nitrogen cycle
with a few LPs under your arm. I said he wasn't in, but you knew.

I was wrapped in a Kimono and a streak of paint. You said I looked
great without no make up and lit up, your fallen halo,
Want to cut my hair, Delilah? The vinyl crackled, you asked,
ash scattered. On the chez lounge I listened to your lament,
didn't believe the things you said. *It's too late to go home.*

I wasn't what you thought, under feathers and flesh and kept
a warning light on. *Can you be in love with more then one girl?*
You asked, serious, my laughter exhaled in your face, glided
to the surface and sang *where did the sane boys slide?*
I put the diamonds in your bag as you flew the morning.

Quel Dommage

This has got to be coded. You deciphered it and no one knew
the answers and we had to pour fixations to the IChing,
song lyrics, patterns birds make in the sky, telegraph wires
wrote your name with the Ogham on leaves. There were secrets,
a hermitic Gematria of losses, records spun revolutions as the Earth.
Tree sister, brother wind, walked from Elephant and Castle
to Holloway in the storm to say you needed me. We made up
codes in the kitchen, eggs meant sex, lightning was love,
you had a key and could lock me up, ate omelettes for breakfast.
We made a collage of us in a cartoon flat. Batman and Joker,
In Arkham together, these things meant something. You looked
at my breasts with your dark glasses on. We made our home
like Vietnam, napalm wallpaper. I wasn't your sister. Comic book
clues turn our pages, I turned to the world and you, in motley,
drowned on the steps of Covent Garden, playing the crowd
for a few pennies. I must write in code because the truth is painful.
I stopped watching you that summer, the game was too truthful,
Hurt sewn into patterns and prophesies. When the codes broke
there were smashed eggs and a lightning crack and I was free.
But you warned me of pain. It came. One night, after you died,
you apologised, and asked me to scratch your name into the leaves
with notches and strokes, a language for the children of trees.

Broke

You said you loved me, Impossible Boy, we'd only just met,
you said you wanted to be my dog and I let you lap,

Animal boy, I never let on that night I was secretly Iggy Pop.
You said I was hot and cold girl, blowing bites like September,

I was pout and preen, weaned in a glamour with a swagger,
blissed in the club. I span you, Top-boy, tales of the end

of the world, told you I'd make magic in a champagne glass
and line of coke. I wanted to forget where I was heading,

coral lips, brittle and deadly. Of course I didn't love you,
how easy to un-cure the heart of heat, be covered in tiger musk.

How easy to leave stink at the tube station, not take calls
or objections. Hard light in nightclubs had me in focus,

you were token, a heart break broken, how easy to lie awake
and leave you wanting more. That's it Happening boy,

my scar your wound and I learned what it is to be fuel.
I was sound of car alarm one night. How easy to be cruel.

Wash Your Hands

The man who locks the door is strong and bold,
doesn't care she's lost a purse or friends.
He doesn't need charming words, doesn't need to flatter
and there a nightclub smoke machine in his jacket.

He's got an unfurled flag in his pocket, —she's a girl
that won't forgive him. She's Lucy Locket with her habit,
and wishes she'd forget it. He's got teeth-sharp eyes
for a girl in a fix. She spins him a line, rips her dress.

He's got other people's problems, he's a mess, and doesn't
have the the time. She's a wild thing in a rush
to feel his charming words, she's a girl, a wood-nymph
in unlit streets, *the least I can do is call you a cab.*

The taxi driver runs by like a day in September,
and doesn't care there's no food on the table when he gets
back, he's got pulled up by the police for that. She says
what's a nice boy like you doing in that burning bed?

The man who locks the door is a man of few words.
She thinks of *Red Hot Chilli Peppers* and a song
in her head about serial killers. He doesn't care that's she's lost
her money, friends, pavements, buildings, rooms, hands.

The Portent

One day he takes everything down, his beads and bangles, takes his face off.
Says nothing exists but you as he sits in the moon's rays

and waits for the records to flip. One day she expects Comet West to appear,
from far North, shining and wild eyed, ready for the morning's electric blue sky.

One day she stays up all night to watch his dazzle, tail spin and coma.
She sees him outgas, surpass himself as he unbuckles,

falls through leaves, flies to the horizon. Somewhere from a basement
he plays a guitar of rock dust, light pressure and water ice.

From earth her eyes dart from side to side to follow his blaze. He doesn't see her
going cold, chart a course, find a map of space to point out

where he goes, all crazed on the radio waves. One day she makes sense
of his punch-drunk songs as he flies too near to the sun.

One day she might predict his return, burned out in a shower of meteorites.
One day she'll take everything down, her naked eyes and records.

Copy Cats

I say the stupidest things and believe her,
holed up on a marzipan mountain,
she makes sheep's eyes at me.
That woman, they all say, she says the stupidest things

and look at her, how she laughs and laughs it off–
covered in left overs, piled under all my jackets,
a catalogue of everything in my record collection.
One day, she says, she'll be happier then me.

Matter of fact brooding voice whispers love,
Dress up like a boy all gauche, and 'thin white duke'
one of them wearing my dresses. How she got in
I'll never know, knows what I've been doing.

I will be famous after I'm dead, she says, she kills me,
cameras trained on my flesh. She puts my things on,
in the wrong order, phones from rooms corners.
I say the stupidest things and believe her.

D Flat Minor

He's at the door, she's at the the window
fizzing, ripening plump, visible, winked at.
The pub on the corner, sits gape-clashing
next to the video shop that sells all night booze.

She comes with the flat, no pool, full ashtrays,
tries on clothes and people, her doorman lets them
in. She's in season, upholstered, listens to Harrison
sing Hare Krishna, waves joss sticks at Buddha.

He knows stories above her, damp damage,
mould, rats, who sits under bridges, places to score,
holes in his shoes to stretch, in with a harem,
shall I dance for you? Unveil and perfume?

He can't s stop knocking, walks on Persian carpets,
someone's ceiling. She has a rude awakening,
on a bathroom floor. The doctor gives a six-month
lease, desirable views of water and trees, a balcony,

deposit, five-by-three garden, and she panics
about defrosting, hears them knocking, hard wood,
pine wood, chip wood, plaster board, Norwegian wood,
self assembly friends, a door bell heart, no answer.

The Boys.

They always lie. You slide next to my seat,
ask for a cigarette and I keep smoking.
All I want to know is where you're sleeping,
I write down all your good points, *clever, handsome,
funny.* I do this while you're not looking.

Do you go to the oaks, poison ash, in hog plum?
In your palm trees in crazy sun? Your stories
make me cry. You didn't know your own name
until you were nine, answered to *Bwoy.* After work
I go and sleep in a tree, in the pines

maybe, in Regent's Park. Over coffee at lunch
we complain about the cold, and compare skin.
They'll always lie, you tell me, *the boys,* you tell me
not to fall for their tricks, call me *funny thing.*
I see you shiver as you sit too close to me, call me

girl, I shouldn't be alone. You will show me
a Calabash, a Cannonball Tree. I say I like the pines
and you laugh, you know Indian trees are pretty
in the monsoon, and I pine. Where do you go?

Show me the ink inside my skin. *Don't believe them,*
you whisper, *bright girl, clever girl,* you smoke
my cigarettes, tell me that the boys lie, give me lists
of blues singers. *It was called Black Girl, that song
you love,* you say. You buy me twenty Silk Cut

before you go, and we drink tea in the smoking room.
I'm not brave like you, don't say anything as you wave
in that long fingered way, *don't fall for the lies,
from the tops of trees, keep ahead of the boys.*

Missiles

You hurled yourself at me while I was looking at shinier things.
You lobbed gold disks in my direction, I found them
Did you drop this? You tapped my shoulder and slung
a song by Magazine and I only heard the wind rustling.

We missed each other. You flew to warmth I couldn't offer,
Waved, your silk paisley shirt at the airport, billowed
about your frame. By the time I remembered,
you were married to a girl more self absorbed then me.

That summer you returned, you took me to happenings
in Hornsey galleries, late night Hoxton bars, poetry readings,
tripped us into some night music where you told me I'd missed
my chance and you were smug because I said I missed you.

Smashing

Flashbulbs and wild card's go off, and the tune won't stop pulsing.
Let's go to the club, the pub, the gig at the Garage.
The top's off, tights' get loose and she's rearranged.
Her foot taps, spine snaps, she can tip tap there in the bright lights.
A hand on her thigh, a sliding glance, arms wide and she's turns Hecate.

She mouths spells to Aphrodite, Dionysus, Tiaco and Pamela Anderson
as her hair curls, lips pout. She's unbuttoned, unzipped and upfront,
She holds onto the stage, sips tequila, mescal and absinthe, makes
mistakes in slow motion. Why not be young-flesh bedazzled for the boys
who urge to spill it in the night club as she belly-dances.

Filaments are sparked while her skins' glass blown and hot, he's moth
ready in the strobe-bright magnetised to her hip-swell. His big shoulders
find their way, sprout feathers to the moon, and turns into wings.
She beckons music, drives faster, spreads her pale skin-veins
and antennae, and he smashes into her light-bulb again, again until
daylight.

Love Craft

Comic caper, dressed like the Velvets, gave himself haircuts
and false names. *Pick this card, stick it in the fridge to keep it
the coolest trick.* A Waterloo Sunset while he sipped
cola in a Soho bar. London cooled, he met her at the bus stop
on Islington Green, St James' park, a party on Caledonian Road.
He met her in the Samuel Becket , pretended he wasn't looking,
Call me the devil, the horned one. Could explain herself on a night bus
to Clerkenwell, sometimes Baudelaire, other times beer
and jellied eels. It was his turn, *what a co-incidence,* he said,
Primal Scream, football, Oasis and cocaine, he offered her Molly
and thirty quid. Cartoon girlfriend, she wept tears *Oh Brad.
Won't you take me out?* She tired, the bands waned and the mixer
didn't fix her, *play me a torch song,* she didn't like his answer,
or his reveal, *You can be Betty Blue and I can be Walter Mitty.*
In the heat of a new, improved city, where the bands played
footie on top of HMV, she took the card from up her sleeve,
said she wanted something real, rubbed him out.

Cherry-Bomb

That old Mae West thing was brought out when needed.
Tattered feather bower, fur coats and what have you.
Curry flavoured little madam, Phoolan Devi, cholan,

and he, not quite James Dean, liked the spices, the colours,
she tasted jellied eels, cockney good-boy shtick,
and special offers. *Shall we play ration books and gravy?*

He did have a lot of books on war, and an active duty
interest in the snipers on the Russian front. *Little boys
want to be soldiers,* was reprimanded with lectures,
the doodlebugs and upkeeps, for his *cherry-bomb.*

G.I. Joe some nights, collar turned up, smoking Lucky
Strikes and found her singing alone in an old vaudeville bar.
He didn't look in the clean up kit, with the Doughboys
tucked in his mess, that bitter morning after.

Record Collection

I hid my music from you, I didn't want you to look, at my record collection,
I knew you could read me like a book, but you'd no recollection.

Lone wolf on the edge of the moon, you held me tighter then a Beatles
hook you didn't know, that day in June, I last played my record collection.

I tried to forget music and words, for many reasons. You fed me your blood,
said you'd read my diaries, scrap books, kept safe with my record collection.

That winter you vowed to keep me warm, sheltered, siphoned my past.
We were fated to buy a home that shook, as I put away my record collection

in a cupboard where I never looked. That hot summer we slept in the garden,
you costumed drapes, lights, incense, made us a Turkish souk, a fine collection

of your strong white limbs, my dark skin, you said we'd blend together well,
but I was scared that I was such a crook, unreal without my record collection.

To you music was irrelevant. You cleared out my cupboards, but I'd overlooked
to say it was part of me, returned to find you'd thrown out my record collection.

Some of Them Are Old
(after Brian Eno)

A back catalogue. The songs came back. *Write me down*, you demand imme-
diately. I'm the masterpiece, remember me? That day in June we flew too
close to the sun, hairstyles catching fire, those brilliant records are all now
on Spotify.

Now we're too far gone. Make arrangements and you turn up, bewildered
like Rip Van Winkle, stains, fag butts and give ups. I haven't heard
that song in thirty years I say. It's too familiar, bites through eye teeth.

We go through our old songs, you kept some, I threw some away.
Let's go see them again because they are alive and keep playing. Some thing old,
still alive, some of them are new. Teenagers in the room, making play

lists on our lips. Take off again once you've turned the corner, shoot 'em up
kid, *get a pod cast*, let everyone hear what you've got to say. Those old songs
stored in your head. The other half of that record collection, completed orbit.

Gentleman Caller

Saturday night's dead dark time,
just the shine of curved backlight bounced
of a metal can, sulks into the left overs,
the egg curry's last dregs. I have left tumeric
stains and I mutter, do I care?
There is a legend that I was once from India,
before the world was so broken
and left scraps of me here in the kitchen.
I throw the night door open,
listening for him, somewhere behind the fox
call, there is laughter, a rattle, fly-catcher,
over here, his tight trick and urgent call,
ticks from his guts, *come here, come here.*
Night singer, I didn't hear over the noises.
The television, the cooker, next door's moans.
I'm leaning from the window as he reaches
quietly at first, and can I answer, tell him
I'm here, at last, ready to duet, into a blank
and deadly future. There is a legend
that nightingales sang for the Indian Kings.
Can I entice him with the smells of spice
and my brown feathers appear, for a moment
as he sings more urgent, now night-jar,
in the coal dark. *Come here, come here.*
Could I shed these fake leopard-skin slippers
and run into the garden, Ovid-charmed,
alarm called, sprout beak and shrink eye,
grow lung-song sharp and he keeps calling,
come, come, and my human hunger is marked,
for his words to sing our lonely songs
from a kitchen window forever in the dead of dark,
fly-catcher, rattler, all my island's voices, *call again.*

The Playlist

https://open.spotify.com/playlist/0SQwrDxHK3jhHL91yVq-JQY?si=CVdRd6rDSqyC7h3qUD8Hng

Acknowledgements

Many thanks to the editors of Marble, Under the Radar, Molly Bloom, Poetry Wales, Ink Sweat and Tears where a number of these poems were first published. Thanks also to Candlestick Press where Hero Worship appears in their Spring edition. Thanks to all the beautiful people who inspired a poem in this book and the songs they inspired me to listen to that became my own playlist. I want to acknowledge all my favourite song writers and musicians, from Bowie, Lou, Iggy, Bryan to REM, so many … who also kept me company over the years, inspired poems and continue to delight me.

Thanks also to Aaron Kent – for being a brilliant editor.

Play Out Your Unrest